YOUR WORD POWER

USING YOUR GOD-GIVEN WORD POWER

ROBIN THOMPSON

Published by:
R.H. Publishing
3411 Preston Rd. Ste. C-13-146
Frisco, Texas 75034

Copyright © 2020, Robin Thompson
ISBN#978-1-945693-47-2

All rights reserved under International Copyright Law. Written permission must be secured from the publisher to reproduce, copy, or transmit any part of this book.

Unless otherwise marked, all Scripture quotations are taken from the NIV, HOLY BIBLE, NEW INTERNATIONAL VERSION®. Copyright © 1973, 1978, 1984 by International Bible Society. Used by permission of Zondervan Bible Publishing House. All rights reserved.

Scriptures marked NLT are taken from the HOLY BIBLE, NEW LIVING TRANSLATION (NLT): Scriptures taken from the HOLY BIBLE, NEW LIVING TRANSLATION, Copyright© 1996, 2004, 2007 by Tyndale House Foundation. Used by permission of Tyndale House Publishers, Inc., Carol Stream, Illinois 60188. All rights reserved. Used by permission.

Scriptures marked NASB are taken from the NEW AMERICAN STANDARD (NASB): Scripture taken from the NEW AMERICAN STANDARD BIBLE®, copyright© 1960, 1962, 1963, 1968, 1971, 1972, 1973, 1975, 1977, 1995 by The Lockman Foundation. Used by permission.

Scriptures marked ESV are taken from the THE HOLY BIBLE, ENGLISH STANDARD VERSION (ESV): Scriptures taken from THE HOLY BIBLE, ENGLISH STANDARD VERSION ® Copyright© 2001 by Crossway, a publishing ministry of Good News Publishers. Used by permission.

Scriptures marked TLB are taken from the THE LIVING BIBLE (TLB): Scripture taken from THE LIVING BIBLE copyright© 1971. Used by permission of Tyndale House Publishers, Inc., Carol Stream, Illinois 60188. All rights reserved.

Scriptures marked TM are taken from the THE MESSAGE: THE BIBLE IN CONTEMPORARY ENGLISH (TM): Scripture taken from THE MESSAGE: THE BIBLE IN CONTEMPORARY ENGLISH, copyright©1993, 1994, 1995, 1996, 2000, 2001, 2002. Used by permission of NavPress Publishing Group

Scripture quotations noted KJV are from The Holy Bible, KING JAMES VERSION.

Scriptures marked NKJV are taken from the NEW KING

JAMES VERSION (NKJV): Scripture taken from the NEW KING JAMES VERSION®. Copyright© 1982 by Thomas Nelson, Inc. Used by permission. All rights reserved.

DEDICATION

This book is dedicated to my two sons Tyrone and Jahmil, and to my family and love ones, that they will find the wisdom, knowledge and the love of God in the secret place, to fight the good fight of faith, to walk in freedom and victory.

Also to all who fight for change, and all who hope and dream for better, I dedicate this book to you. For all to believe in the power of their words for transformation, change and victory in Jesus name.

I dedicate this book to every prayer warrior, leader, teacher, friend who has poured into my life to stand firm on God's Word, that if nothing else, just stand.

I dedicate this book to you to believe again that all things are subject to change through prayer. I dedicate this book to all who have truly surrendered their life to Christ for the sharing of the gospel that others may know Him and have salvation. I honor you today for your dedication and your sacrifice for God's glory.

For those who have gone before us, warred on our behalf and plowed the way, I thank you, we thank you, and bless you!

TABLE OF CONTENTS

INTRODUCTION	9
YOU CAN DO IT	11
IN THE BEGINNING	15
DEATH AND LIFE	19
BY YOUR WORDS	23
TAMING THE TONGUE	27
THE TONGUE IS FIRE	31
PROTECT YOUR MOUTH	35
OUT OF THE HEART	39
BLESSINGS AND CURSINGS	43
EQUIPPED	47
SWORD OF THE SPIRIT	51
FAITH — HEAR — SPEAK	55
CALLING THINGS FORTH/SPEAKING THINGS INTO EXISTENCE	59
SHALL NOT RETURN EMPTY	63

SPEAK IT — SAY IT — PROPHESY..................67

PRAISES GO UP, BLESSINGS COME DOWN..........71

OPEN YOUR MOUTH..................75

SPEAKING UP FOR OTHERS..................77

TELL IT TO MOVE..................81

HEALING WORDS..................85

BUILDING WORDS..................89

SWEET WORDS..................93

WISDOM..................97

KNOWLEDGE..................101

SELF-CONTROL..................105

WAIT..................109

THE RIGHT ANSWER..................111

DON'T COMPLAIN..................115

DON'T LIE..................119

DON'T GOSSIP..................123

BLESS THEM..................125

INTRODUCTION

YOUR WORD POWER is all about using the power of your words from a biblical principle for advancing the Kingdom of God—let your word power transform your world.

The year is 2020. The year 5780 on the Hebrew calendar. This is the year of Peh, which means the mouth. This is the year, era, the decade of the mouth, a decade of declaration, the voice, what you speak, having the power of life and death. This is the era to use your voice like never before—to rise up. Don't agree with what you see. Speak and decree change.

God said, "Open your mouth and I will fill it." It's time to prophesy and to speak to those dry bones. It's time for supernatural movement and change. There's power that God wants to release to you, through your words, and what you speak.

Listen to your mouth! Your mouth measures your faith. There are so many teachings on the power of your words, but guess what, it never gets old, it's a "right-now-word."

This book is a self-help devotional with 31 days of prayer and decrees to push you forward into using your word power. No one can speak for you, like you; no one can tell your story, like you; no one can fight for you, like you, and that's why God gave you a mouth to speak, to use your word power that comes out of your mouth.

I know for myself to overcome obstacles in life, I have to apply the Word of God and Scripture. It gives me strength. It gives me faith to fight, knowing I already have the victory through JESUS Who died on the cross for me, that I could be free from sin, that His blood was shed for you and for me, that I would have life.

Your word power is your power to transform your life, your family, your finances, your health, your business, education, city, town ... you name it. You have the power. There is power that God wants to release to you, through your very own word power for transformation and change.

Let's enjoy the journey of being an overcomer, walking in victory by speaking and using our very own word power. Speak to those things that are not, as though they are. It's time to prophesy, to speak to those dry bones, and live. You're called to be powerful, and God wants you to believe you are Who He says you are.

DAY 1: YOU CAN DO IT!

Philippians 4:13: "I can do all things through Christ who strengthens me."

Isaiah 41:10: "So do not fear, for I am with you; do not be dismayed, for I am your God. I will strengthen you and help you; I will uphold you with my right hand.

I know for some of you, reading the cover of this book YOUR WORD POWER, can maybe be intimidating, and you're like, "I can do it," and then you're like, "Can I do it?" and then you say, "I am not sure I can do it. Can my vocabulary ever be changed to such a positive voice of speaking? And for others you're saying, "No problem, I got this, this is a breeze for me."

Well I encourage you to pray for the ones who are struggling with believing in themselves for change ... for disciplining their tongue, mouth and words.

Roman 12:2: "Do not conform to the pattern of this world, but be transformed by the renewing of your mind. Then you will be able to test and approve what God's will is-his good, pleasing and perfect will."

I encourage you to take this journey to the road of extraordinary change. Growth is change, and change is growth, but to stay the same is death. Trust and have faith in God and don't give up—you will be transformed.

I believe in you. God truly believes in you, and all of Heaven rejoices because they believe in you. So let's do it! Your voice needs to be heard right now! Your word power needs to be spoken an activated for God's Blessing and change to take place in Heaven and on Earth.

Matthew 19:26: "But Jesus looked at them and said, 'with man this is impossible, but with God all things are possible.'"

May God, our Heavenly Father, bless you and keep you and shine his face upon you.

QUESTION: Will you ask God to help you get through this new journey of forever using your own word power? How will this help you?

PRAYER: Father God, I pray that my eyes look up to heavens, that You continuously lift my head up, even when it is too heavy for me; help me to look up to You for strength, that You will release an open Heaven over me, that this time my life will be transformed. Singing that old song, "I have decided to follow Jesus. No turning back, no turning back!

DECREE: I can do all things through Christ Who strengthens me, that I will walk in faith and that He is my rock, my strong foundation that I will not be moved, that God will be with me every step of the way, and I will be transformed.

I decree I will complete this study to the very end, and I will fight and persevere until all my strength is gone. I will not give up, knowing that I have partnered with my Heavenly Father, and I will finish strong in Jesus name.

Notes

DAY 2: IN THE BEGINNING

John 1:1-5 "In the beginning was the Word, and the Word was with God, and the Word was God. He was with God in the beginning. Through him all things were made; without him nothing was made that has been made. In him was life, and that life was the light of all mankind. The light shines in the darkness, and the darkness has not overcome it."

In the beginning was the Word of God—from the very start, was His word. Wow! God is full of mysteries.

Majestic in all His ways. God spoke and it was so. God spoke and it was created; it was alive, awakened and birthed, brought forth by His Word. And it was good in God eyes.

The Word is one of many of the greatest gifts God has given to you and me to prosper. The Word of God is our personal blueprint to a godly, righteous and blessed life, so that we may have a hope and a future ... and obtain all the promises and blessing of God. He wants so much for us to succeed and to be blessed, but we must go after it, fight for it and partner with Him on the journey.

FYI: you cannot do it alone. You need God's help. He will meet you right where you are at. His hand is reaching out for you to take it, grab it and don't let go of His mighty hand.

Jeremiah 29:11 "'For I know the plans I have for you,' declares the Lord, plans to prosper you and not harm you, plans to give you a hope and a future."

God is a God Who shall not lie. He is a loving God; He is a forgiving God, He is your friend and your Father. Try HIM. Trust Him. Get to know Him, the God Who supplies your every need. The great I AM! "Truth, that comes from the mouth of God.'" This is what we must stand on, it is our solid rock foundation.

I invite you today to study, speak, teach and share the Word of God. It is an open invitation to you and all the world for you to sit at His table and partake of His Word and truth, that your eyes would be opened and the veil be removed, taste and see His goodness. Speak—open your mouth, use your very own God-given Word power to be made whole and new in Christ Jesus. I am so excited for you; this is going to be a truly awesome experience, so let's get started.

QUESTION: Will you ask God to reveal Himself to you in a new way, revealing His Word power? How will this help you?

PRAYER: Lord, bless me to learn, stand and retain Your Word and truth. Give me a fresh revelation of the Word of God, that my word power will be activated as a force of holy fire, piercing hearts, minds, and souls.

DECREE: I am so grateful for the Word of God, and I will take full advantage of its teachings and access all that has been given to me through His Word and apply it to my life, in Jesus name.

Notes

DAY 3: DEATH AND LIFE

Proverbs 18:21 "The tongue has the power of life and death, and those who love it will eat its fruit."

"Words kill, words give life; they're either poison or fruit-you choose. " (TMT)

Time for a Comprehension break! Do you understand what you say and speak have the power of life and death? Your tongue can speak life, freedom, growth and blessings or it can speak death, bondage, and destruction. If we truly understood or had a deeper revelation of the power of our words, we wouldn't be so quick to speak, but always relying and trusting God for His wisdom.

Proverbs 15:28 "The heart of the godly thinks carefully before speaking." (NLT)

Speaking to a matter, situation or a person is so critical because of what you say, and how you say it. The tongue holds so much power—the power of life or death. You're able to give life, breath, a heartbeat to a dead matter.
   Your mouth can release change, begin a shift, bring life forth ... you choose.
   Or you can bring death, destruction, and deterioration ... you choose.

I choose life. I hope you do, too. Choose your words carefully; wait for a moment, think, ponder and pray before speaking.

As you walk into this enjoy the fruit of it; there is much fruit in speaking life and God wants you to reap the harvest of your words. God always gives us a choice in life, even when it comes to receiving Him as our Lord and Savior. This is a choice you make; it is up to you, never being forced upon you. Know that the Holy Spirit is a gentlemen waiting for you. The choice is yours; you can speak fruit and life or speak death and destruction—words that hinder, blind, and stunt growth.

Let's choose life and fruit, bringing forth the beautiful things of God's original intent for mankind. Know YOUR words have that much power, to change an entire nation, to birth something or destroy it. I want to encourage you that there is hope for all things, as God has given us the authority to speak, so you will speak, for your family, for world change, for God's will.

The hope and the change starts with you as you open your mouth to pray and to decree that change is taking place. God has given you a mouth, a voice, and a tongue; all to speak, to have dominion on earth, for the Kingdom of God. So partner with God and the heavens and speak life for His glory.

QUESTION: Will you ask God for His help today to speak life and not death? How will this help you?

PRAYER: God, I love You, and I am so sorry for the effects of my words that may have caused any harm to me or others. I take them back. I cancel any death words in Jesus' name. Please forgive me for not always speaking life; I repent. Help me to speak only life and eat its fruit. Help me to prophesy life, that living waters may flow to everyone I come in contact with, leaving fruitful seeds for a great harvest in Jesus' name.

DECREE: Lord, I will Speak life from my tongue—life into others, my family, my children, my spouse, loved ones, neighbors, leadership, business, jobs, schools, churches, government, and to my city, state, and nation in Jesus' name.

Notes

DAY 4: BY YOUR WORDS

Matthew 12:37 "For by your words you will be acquitted, and by your words you will be condemned."

Matthew 12:37 "Let me tell you something: Every one of these careless words is going to come back to haunt you. There will be a time of Reckoning." (TM)

Words are powerful; take them seriously. Words can be your salvation. Words can also be your damnation. Your words can be freedom or bondage, life or death. Yes, by your word you can cause serious action or serious consequences. Let's really think about this in our day-to-day lifestyle.

Have you ever had someone tell you that you could not accomplish something or not give you the proper creditability you deserve? Not aware of their actions or what they are saying or doing, they have just tried to imprison you with that thought. In some way or form, subconsciously those words have influenced your mind and thoughts, almost trapping you or putting a snare on you.

In another form one can say, yes, go after your dreams. I believe in you; you can do this. With these words you have just set that person free, to freely think, believe and dream again; to do the best they can and go after it, that's blessing one with freedom. It's that simple using your word power, prison or freedom, death or life blessings or curses, you choose. God has called us to set the captive free.

Note to self: One shouldn't let another's opinion of approval or disapproval effect your decisions or destiny. We don't want to be captive by one's words—we want freedom!
Never receive or agree with words, if they don't line up with the Word of God for your life and if they don't resonate with your spirit. If you're unsettled, uneasy, keep seeking God for answers.
He sends confirmations through His Word, people, songs and many other ways. Keep watching, keep your eyes open and your ears listening. He is always speaking.

QUESTION: How will you use your word power starting today? How will this help you?

PRAYER: Father God, You're beautiful and wonderful to me. Please forgive me and whatever effects my words may have done to damage others. I repent for every careless word I have ever spoken. Lord, please create in me a new man who speaks boldly from the thrown of God. Where my words are not harmful, but a force of mighty power, speaking blessings from the Father's heart, in Jesus' name.

DECREE: My words are powerful and I will use them as a powerful force of representing change and positive transformation to speak blessings and what is good and pleasing to the Lord.

Notes

DAY 5: TAMING THE TONGUE

James 3:8 "But no human being can tame the tongue. It is a restless evil, full of deadly poison."

Have you ever said something you did not want to say, and you could not take it back? Then asking yourself, "Why did I say that? Where did that come from?" This proves how easily words can slip off of our tongues.

James 3:8 "No man can tame the tongue."

It is only obtained through the power of God that one can walk in such a discipline. With God's help, we can walk through this journey in victory. You can become victorious through Christ Jesus, Who is faithful above all things. You can be free of speaking too quickly and living with regrets of what you have said—not giving time to processing your thoughts and how they may effect someone.
God is all powerful, all knowing he knows your struggles and how much you want to change. And surely He knows how to help and direct your path, order your steps, making every crocked place straight.

Psalm 139:4 "Even before there is a word on my tongue, Behold O LORD, You know it all." (NASB)

Your tongue can be tamed through God's anointing power, and trusting, and believing Him to do so. God wants this more for you than yourself. He is like "Yes, just ask Me. Ask, knock, seek and find.

John 14:14 "If you ask me anything in my name, I will do it."

1 Chronicles 16:11 "Look to the Lord and his strength; seek his face always."

1 Peter 3:10 "For, 'Whoever would love life and see good days must keep their tongue from evil and their lips from deceitful speech.'"

Seeking God daily will help you develop a disciplined tongue. Do not be discouraged. There is a new beginning every morning. A fresh start.

    Bishop T D Jakes always says, "You can win if you do not quit." Do not quit, keep trying; keep your eyes on God for He makes all things new. By His strength you will be transformed. God can give you a new language, a new tongue, a new love language to speak and communicate with, an understanding to everyone's particular needs.

    God is with you. He has already commanded His angels to take charge and cover over you. He will give you the strength and strategy to overcome the biggest obstacles of your life, you will be a testimony!

QUESTION: Will you ask God to help you to tame your tongue starting today? How will this help you?

PRAYER: My God, my Father, the faithful One, Your mercy is new every morning, starting fresh and new. Help me to tame my tongue. Help me to be disciplined in my speaking. Remove any evil from my mouth, and give it a cleansing in Jesus' name.

DECREE: I will walk with a tamed and disciplined tongue, through the strength of Christ Jesus.

Notes

DAY 6: THE TONGUE IS FIRE

James 3:5 "Likewise, the tongue is a small part of the body, but it makes great boasts. Consider what a great forest is set on fire by a small spark. The tongue also is a fire, a world of evil among the parts of the body. It corrupts the whole person, sets the whole course of his life on fire, and it itself set on fire by hell."

Hot and heated you have become because of your tongue. Your, body burns, your head aches, you skin turns flush. You are so furious that you could just about say anything out of your mouth! It's there, bubbling up, like burning hot water. And just like when hot water hits your body, it burns, causing pain, permanent scares, needing a long recovery time. It's devastating and unforgettable.

Everything you thought, everything you have been holding in, holding back, it is now coming out. Don't burn in anger and rage because of your mouth, your feelings and emotions. If you continue to operate in life on feelings and emotions, you will be constantly defeated, conquered, and destroyed!

Your tongue is a weapon, ready for war or peace. Don't let those guys (feelings and emotions) win! Don't let them set the course of destiny. You're giving them too much power over your life. People have lost jobs and great opportunities because they are titled too emotional.

What a disappointing way to lose an opportunity because they can't trust you with your up and down, emotional roller coaster that you display time after time. People are watching you; judging you character; believe it and keep your eyes open and look around you. You will see the eyes looking upon you. You may say you don't care who's watching you, it doesn't matter, but God is watching and He wants you to be great and whole, and you are representing Him through it all. You can't trust your emotions. They will deceive you and others. Making you unqualified!

Jeremiah 23:29 "'Is not my word like fire,' declares the Lord, 'and like a hammer that breaks a rock in pieces?'"

God set a great example of His Word being as a fire and a hammer, breaking up things. So we must ask God to set the course of our tongue.

QUESTION: Will you ask God starting today to help you with your feelings and emotions? How would this benefit your life moving forward?

PRAYER: God, I bless Your holy name. You are the great I AM. I need Your help for changes in my life, to remove the things that may be holding me back. Help me with my feelings and emotions so that I will have victory over my tongue and over all of myself in Jesus' name.

DECREE: I will overcome operating out of my emotions and feelings. I will conquer my tongue.

Notes

DAY 7: PROTECT YOUR MOUTH

Psalm 141:3 "Set a guard over my mouth, O Lord; keep watch over the door of my lips."

Proverbs 21:23 "Those who guard their mouths and their tongues keep themselves from calamity."

Ever heard the term, "Watch your mouth?" We know in life that things can be said quicker than in the blink of an eye. Things we can't take back sometimes. You're shocked that you even said it. And sorry you cannot take those words back. They cannot be erased. You can say sorry and apologize as many times you like, but it doesn't change the fact that you said it and that person heard it. It is recorded in their brain with a non-delete button.

    Really being unaware of knowing how much power your words have, releases a furry of fire. Do you really know? How much pain have you caused and how will this effect someone? What damage have you done ... maybe releasing hurt, wounds in another life that could take a lifetime to heal? When those bad words hit, destruction starts to take set. Those words try to become a part of who you are. They attack your charter, self-esteem, and your self-worth. Causing meatal confusion.

    Don't let those negative words have that much power over you, especially when you are the one in charge with God's power and authority. Pressing forward, let's guard our mouth from using ugly words and guard our ears from hearing and receiving those ungodly, negative destructive words from entering into our hearts.

Proverbs 29:20 "Do you see a man who is hasty in his words? There is more hope for a fool then him."

Let us be the example of greatness as we guard our mouth with the help of God. Let's take baby steps to pause, ponder and pray, meditate on His Word daily so that before we speak, it is sweet, and that your words will be released with love, compassion, understanding and God's grace.

Proverbs 13:3 "Whoever guards his mouth preserves his life; he who opens wide his lips come's to ruin."

God wants us to walk in this discipline and self-control that brings a new respect, honor and trust.

QUESTION: Will you ask God today to help you protect your mouth? How will this help you?

PRAYER: Father God, help me to guard my mouth, that I may walk and be an example of Who You are, as we display discipline, wisdom and most importantly, love in Jesus' name.

DECREE: You Lord have set a guard over my mouth and a door over my lips. Nothing that is not pleasing to You will come out of my mouth.

Notes

DAY 8: OUT OF THE HEART

Matthew 15:18 "But the things that come out of the mouth come from the heart, and these make a man 'unclean.'"

Matthew 6:21 "For where your treasure is, there your heart will be also."

Jeremiah 17:9 "The heart is deceitful above all things and desperately sick; who can understand it." (ESV)

Proverbs 4:23 "Above all else, guard your heart for everything you do flow from it."

Proverbs 27:19 "As water reflects the face, so one's life reflects the heart."

The heart and the mouth are aligned. What is in the heart comes out of the mouth. The heart speaks out so much about you. God knows all, and He knows your heart. You can't fool Him; He see right through your flesh to the depth of your soul.
    Have you ever heard people say, "God knows my heart?" Oh yes, He does, and maybe that's the problem. Maybe your heart can even deceive you, blinding you from hidden truth, and deception. Well, God is the fixer-upper.

He is the Holy maintenance man. Just put in your request. He is ready to cleanse your heart and mind, making all things new, Holy and acceptable unto Him. This needs to take place so that you are set free, so moving forward you won't have any 'stinking thinking,' and your heart won't be full of deception—becoming delusional, leading you down the wrong path. God makes every crocked place straight in your life, just trust Him.

None of us are perfect; that is why we need God's help to make us better, a better you, one day at a time. Or He can do a mighty, quick work, happening in an instant. Give it all to Him so he can set you free. Truly, we have to continuously examine ourselves. There may be something hidden in your heart that needs to be removed, that we may not see. Just ask God, and He will show you, revealing all hidden things.

Surely He can set you free if you ask HIM. This will help you to start speaking peacefully, with joy, releasing happiness and goodness across the land. This is God's desire for you. He will heal your heart, removing all fragmented and shattered pieces, removing any ungodly arrows and darts out of your heart, removing all bad residue so that you may be healed and whole in Christ Jesus.

Matthew 9:4 "But Jesus, knowing their thoughts, said, 'Why do you think evil in your hearts?'" (ESV)

Psalm 44:21 "Would not God find this out? For He knows the secrets of the heart." (NASB)

QUESTION: Will you ask God today to do a quick work in your heart, to cleanse and heal it? How will this help you?

PRAYER: Purify my heart, make it brand new, and cleanse my heart so that what flows out of it is pure and true. Let my heart only reflect You, Your love, mercy and grace. Teach me, Lord, to guard my heart, but in a healthy way, so that Your love flows in and out in Jesus' name.

DECREE: You, Lord, are the treasure of my heart. My heart will reflect You and only You. Living waters flow from my heart.

Notes

DAY 9: BLESSINGS AND CURSES

James 3:9-10 "With the tongue we praise our Lord and Father, and with it we curse human beings, who have been made in God's likeness. Out of the same mouth come praise and cursing. My brothers, this should not be."

Yes, Brothers and Sisters this should not be; that we can use the very thing to bless and curse, operating out of our own emotions, emotions and feelings that cannot be trusted. Emotions like: fear, lack, misunderstanding, misinterpreting, speaking negatively, speaking out of anger, jealously, envy, strife or spite. Such a dangerous place to dance around in, taking you to places you should not be, sliding into delusion, and deception, being unable to make wise decisions.

Stand on this. Know what God has for you is for you. No one can take it from you; no one can do it better then you, because that's what God has assigned to you. It's yours! So, go after it, grab hold of it, and don't look to the right or the left, that's a distraction. Stay in your lane until the assignment is complete.

If we truly get the revelation of speaking blessings and curses upon one another's lives, this will be a game changer in your life. Curses, causing harm, or trying to bring punishment and misery upon someone, speaking bad, ill wishes, not understanding how this can effect someone, even harboring the thoughts of evil. Yes, I said evil, to covet another man's blessing, is a sin.

God has a blessing with your name on it. A plan and a purpose designed just for you, so don't trip, be patient. We can desire the same blessings as others, but we must do what it takes to reap the harvest, the work that it takes to get it, not taking, stealing or operating in a robbing spirit, wanting one or cursing their God-given blessing is not of God. Understand when you speak blessings, you're releasing the supernatural things of God through His Word. You're releasing God's favor and protection by using your word power, by opening up your mouth to speak, partnering with God to release His Word, His blessings through your mouth.

But be encouraged. Biblically, in any religion, it teaches you the important of speaking blessings—blessings over your family, loved ones, and others. As you speak these blessings they are taking life-form, being activated and starting to manifest in Jesus' name. Be sure to release numerous, uncountable blessings over yourself, family, friends, loved ones and others. They will be blessed by the words of your lips. They will be blessed by your very own word power.

Deuteronomy 28:8 "The Lord will send a blessing on your barns and on everything you put your hands to. The Lord your God will bless in the land he is giving you."

Proverbs 10:22 "The blessing of The Lord brings wealth, and he adds no trouble to it."

Ephesians 1:3 "Praise be the God and Father of our Lord Jesus Christ, who has blessed us in the heavenly realms with every spiritual blessing in Christ."

QUESTION: Will you ask God to help you to speak only blessings and not curses? How will this help you?

PRAYER: Father God, please forgive me if I have spoken any curses unknowingly. I repent of any harm I may have done out of ignorance. Bless me, Lord, to use my mouth for supernatural blessings in Jesus' name.

DECREE: I will speak blessings and not curses. I will use my word power for speaking blessings unlimited over myself and my loved ones and others in Jesus' name.

Notes

DAY 10: EQUIPPED

2 Timothy 3:17 "So that the man of God may be thoroughly equipped for every good work." (KJV)

Philippians 1:6 "Being confident of this, that he who began a good work in you will carry it on to completion until the day of Christ Jesus."

And you may ask yourself, "Why me? Do I have what it takes? Can I do this? Am I qualified? The answer is "Yes." God was reviewing your resume and all your social media accounts, your background check, drug test, your bloodline, your education, you know everything the world uses to disqualify you, God uses it the opposite way, to promote you for His glory. He takes all the dirty laundry and the heavy baggage, the brokenhearted, wounded and starts to heal, mold and reshape you like a piece of clay that's put on the potter's wheel to begin the process of making a new man in Christ.

So, yes, you do have what it takes. So now what? Are you going believe God and go for it, or listen to fear of the enemy that is deeply rooted in you? God says try Me. As you step out, God will meet you. His hand is reaching out to you, take it, commune with Him, talk to Him, cry, let everything go so that now God can began where you end. He has fully equipped you to run this race, supplying you with every tool that you need to win. Just do not give up and don't quit. God will order your steps, showing himself mightily in your life.

Hebrews 13:21 "Equip you in every good thing to do His will, working in us that which is pleasing in His sight, through Jesus Christ, to who be the glory forever and ever. Amen." (NASB)

God wants to teach you some things and guide you through the process. Just for once try him in a new way.

Psalm 32:8 "I will instruct you and teach you in the way you should go; I will counsel you with my loving eye on you."

God is forever watching you. He wants to give you every good thing, but a closed mouth doesn't get fed. So once again open your mouth, tell God your desires, dreams, your plans, your hurts and pains. Tell Him all your secrets, for He is a friend and a good Father. He already knows; He just wants you to share. He wants to hear it from you. Open your mouth and your heart to the Kings of kings. No one said it would be easy. But if God is for you, who can be against you. Be reassured that God is always with you.

Exodus 14:14 "The Lord will fight for you; you need only to be still."

QUESTION: Will you ask the Lord to equip you today to do His great work to speak His Word and share His truth, to release your voice? How will this help you?

PRAYER: Thank You, God, that I have been fully equipped in You. Help me to grow in You, using Your Word, prayer, and praise, as all of this is being released from my mouth for Your glory.

DECREE: I will not quit. I will not give up. I will run this race to completion. God has already equipped me with all that I need.

Notes

DAY 11: THE SWORD OF THE SPIRIT

Ephesians 6:17 "And take THE HELMENT OF SALVATION, and the sword of the Spirit, which is the word of God." (ESV)

Hebrews 4:12 "For the word of God is living and active and sharper than any two edged sword, piercing to the division of soul and of spirit, of joints and of marrow, and discerning the thoughts and intentions of the heart." (ESV)

Read your Bible! I Repeat, read your Bible! I cannot emphasize that enough. I am praying all gain an understanding of the importance of studying the Word of God and how much it will help you, direct you and all the benefits attached to it.

The Word is abundantly full of harvest and blessings, teaching and instructions. That way when you are weak, the Word makes you strong. When the enemy hits you to try and attack you, you're able to stand on the Word of God. In our everyday walk, knowing what the Word says is your weapon. It's a strong, firm foundation, something to stand on that is not shakable or movable.

In our life, we must use the Word of God to fight, to plow through, to press on. This is how we fight our battles. Apply the Word of God and speak it out loud. Let the walls hear you in your home. Let the plants hear. Let the wind of God blow your words right where they need to go. Let your spirit rest in the Word of God. Let the Word bring relief, comfort, protection and reassurance to your life. The Word is so powerful, and today we invite you to go deeper into His Word and that the understanding and revelation be revealed by your Abba Father through His Word.

Matthew 4:4 "But Jesus told him, 'No!' The Scriptures say, 'People do not live by bread alone, but by every word that comes from the mouth of God.'"

Using God's Word and the Scriptures daily is a weapon of mass destruction to the enemy; he is not ready for it. He didn't see it coming, he thought he could take you down easily; he thought he could back you into a corner, thinking you were not alert or prepared. Let's stay ready, so we won't have to get ready, when the time comes; amen.

    Study, level up in your word. Go higher, go after the big things of God.

Psalm 119:130 "The unfolding of your words gives light; it gives understanding to the simple."

Luke 24:45 "Then he opened their minds to understand the Scriptures …" (NLT)

QUESTION: Will you ask God starting today to teach you His Word with an understanding, revealing revelation and truth by the Holy Spirit? How will this help you?

PRAYER: Father, draw me closer to You and Your Word and truth. Help me to go deeper into a new revelation and understanding of Your Word.

DECREE: I will forever use the Word of God in my daily walk and to fight my battles in Jesus' name.

Notes

DAY 12: FAITH—HEAR—SPEAK

Proverbs 18:20 "From the fruit of their mouth a person's stomach is filled; with the harvest of their lips they are satisfied."

Romans 10:17 "So faith comes from hearing, and hearing through the word of Christ." (ESV)

Hebrew 11:1 "Now faith is being sure of what we hope for and certain of what we do not see."

Your mouth releases your faith. Your tongue speaks by faith. Your ears hear by faith. We move in faith every day, knowing and unknowingly, believing for the good things to happen, hoping all goes well. Faith is one of the many gifts from God. As we believe commanding things, we speak a thing, trusting and hoping for a thing. We must move and operate in faith. We must have just enough faith, small as a little tiny mustard seed, to move mountains.

    As God increases our faith daily by building up trust in Him through His word, little by little, the seeds begin to grow and we can stand on the Word of God. We must read His Word. We must start somewhere for the strengthening of our faith. Speaking life requires faith for change. Ask God to increase your faith and vision of Him.

2 Corinthians 4:13 "It is written: 'I believed; therefore I have spoken."

Since we have that same spirit of faith, we also believe and therefore speak. Here are some Scriptures that can help build your faith for you to study. (Luke 8:47) the woman with the issue of blood healed immediately; (Matthew 14:22-33) Jesus walks on the water; (John 9:1-41) healing the blind; (Mark 7: 31-37) healing the deaf man; (John 11:43) Lazarus comes forth from the dead. Now that is walking in phenomenal faith, and the reassurance of who one is in Christ Jesus.

2 Corinthians 5:7 "For we live by faith not by sight."

John 10:27 "My sheep hear my voice, and I know them, and they follow me."

Matthew 11:15 "He who has ears to hear, let him hear."

God wants you to hear Him, listen and learn as He speaks to you. Let Him be your greatest teacher of the Word of God. The author and finisher of our faith.

Ephesians 2:8 "For it is by grace you have been saved, through faith-and this is not from yourselves, it is the gift of God."

Romans 10:8 "But what does it say? The word is near you, in your mouth and in your, heart that is, the word of faith that we proclaim."

QUESTION: Will you ask God to give you the gift of faith, increasing your faith? How will this help you?

PRAYER: We thank, You, God for giving us access to the gift of Faith. Impart in us a fresh download of faith that I can operate in exactly what you predestine me to be, walking in miraculous faith for signs, wonders and miracles.

DECREE: I will operate in the fullness of all THAT Christ Jesus has given to me—speaking to mountains, decreeing things, calling things forth. I will speak things into existence, speaking in faith for healings, etc.

Notes

DAY 13: CALLING THINGS FORTH/ SPEAKING THINGS INTO EXISTENCE

Mark 11:24 "Therefore I tell you, whatever you ask for in prayer, believe that you have received it, and it will be yours."

Job 22:28 "Thou shalt also decree a thing, and it shall be established unto thee: and the light shall shine upon thy ways." (KJV)

Romans 4:17 "(as it is written: 'I have made thee a father of many nations.') In the presence of Him who he believed, even God, who quickeneth the dead and calleth those things which are not, as though they were." (KJV)

If I had a voice, what would I say? What would I do? What would I pray? I would speak for change that burdens my heart. If God gave me a voice, how far would I lift it up—high so high that the heavens would hear my cries? Cries so high that heaven's ears would burn, then change and movement will begin to turn, things will never be the same because the portal is open, breaking every chain.

God gave me a voice which is sweet to His ears. How much does heaven want to possibly hear? God is pleased with such a sweet sound that blessings and overflow start to come down. God says please, please use your voice. I am your God, but you make every choice. I have given free will to man, but I'm here waiting on you and your command—commands to set the captives free and to defeat every enemy.

I am your God with a perfect plan, take the scroll out of My hand, now eat it day and night that your vision and strength will be right, continue to speak on man's behalf and earth and heaven would have great laughs, rejoicing, of joy and victory on how we defeated the enemy, God the Messiah has heard all of your praise, you will hear heaven and earth shout hooray.

God has given you the authority to open up the heavens, to decree a thing, the power to call things forth, to bring things to life, to give it breath, also to speak things into existence, things that are not, as if they were. This is truly speaking by faith, agreeing with God. He teaches us in His Word that once again faith is key to destined change and breakthrough.

We all want change, improvement for something to get better, but sometimes we just don't know where to start, how to begin, or what to do. Well, hallelujah, thank You, JESUS! It's God's Divine plan that you would take time to read this book. This book will definitely help you unlock some things. It will also help you with your verbal exercises to get you speaking. This is not a one-time deal. It's a life-time skill. I encourage you to never, never stop.

Apply it in every area of your life.

Psalm 119:171 "May my lips overflow with praise, for you teach me your decrees ..."

In prayer, if you are still and for long enough, God will speak to you. He will begin to teach you the secret things, in the secret place.

Matthew 13:9 "Who hath ears to hear, let him hear." (KJV)

As previously mentioned, this is the decade, era of the mouth, the year of the voice starts now, the Jewish calendars 5780. (THE YEAR OF THE MOUTH, PEI). One of the meanings of pei is mouth. This should awaken you to focus on your word power more than ever.
    God operates in times and seasons. God and we are in His timing right now. What an awesome time to be in, to effectively speak and expect change; your mouth is your weapon, your words, your declarations, decrees all need to be heard. God is waiting to hear you speak. He is ready to move on your behalf. So speak! Your words reflect and direct your destiny. Use your word power to call things forth. Redirect, take back, claim it, cancel it, move it, stop, reshape our lives, shift things. If you can see it, say it—if you vision it, pull it down from the heavens. Touch and agree with God; it's yours. He has already given it to you. You just have to grab hold of it and take it.

QUESTION: Will you ask God today to be your partner in prayer, to help you to start speaking by faith? How will this help you?

PRAYER: God, please teach me how to speak by faith, beyond my thoughts and comprehension. LORD, help me to reshape my life with my very own word power. Help me to be a force of change, a fresh wind of empowerment, speaking and receiving, believing for supernatural blessing in Jesus' name.

DECREE: When I open my mouth, You will fill it. I will release my voice with faith and authority. I will look at what is beyond me, calling it in, calling it forth, giving it life from my words.

Notes

DAY 14: SHALL NOT RETURN EMPTY

Isaiah 55:11 "So is my word that goes out from my mouth: It will not return to me empty, but will accomplish what I desire and achieve the purpose for which I sent it."

Okay, let's break this down to apples and oranges. God said it, He sent it, it shall not return empty, it will accomplish what He desires, it will achieve the purpose for which He sent it! These are the words of the great I AM—the all, powerful, all knowing. It will happen.

Huge note to self: you are made in God's image, so therefore, you say it, you send it, it shall accomplish, achieve the purpose for which you sent it. In God's timing everything will come to pass, if we believe and operate in faith, using the authority and your word power to speak things forth. Have patience; waiting on the Lord is key to your relationship in Christ.

Ephesians 3:20 "Now to him who is able to do for more abundantly than all that we ask or think, according to the power at work within us," (ESV)

Don't underestimate God or put Him in a box of your own thinking; you only short yourself with limitations. Ask God to expand your thinking of Him that you will grow in Him to shift your paradigm.

Proverbs 3:5 "Trust in the Lord with all your heart and lean not on your own understanding;"

Isaiah 55:8 "'For my thoughts are not your thoughts, neither are your ways my ways,' declares the LORD."

Psalm 33:9 "For he spoke, and it came to be; he commanded, and it stood firm."

Numbers 23:19 "God is not human, that he should lie, not a human being, that he should change his mind. Does he speak and then not act? Does he promise and not fulfill?"

Luke 4:6 "And said to him, 'To you I will give all this authority and their glory, for it has been delivered to me, and I give it to whom I will.'" (ESV)

God is holy; HE is just. God is saying in His Word access granted; it's as if an arrow is being shot to hit a target and it will not miss—guaranteed! That is something to rejoice over. This is one of my favorite Scriptures to share, Isaiah 55:11, because it represents how much power we have in Christ Jesus. To know the power of God's Word will not miss the mark. To know what you speak shall be heard! That makes me fill encouraged to send out the troops with my word power.

God has equipped you to speak; you're made in His image. His Word is on your tongue to decree and declare blessings, create, build, or to tear down and destroy. Speaking life to structures that cannot be moved, strong foundations. Be encouraged to know that when you pray for your community, city, state, and nation things happen. Speak to the seven mountains of influence, local and federal government, media, arts and entertainment, business, education, religion, family, and know that movement is taking place because you opened your mouth.

QUESTION: Will you ask God today to help you believe that He will do what He said? Will you speak a word completely by faith? How will this help you?

2 Corinthians 1:20 "For no matter how many promises God has made, they are "Yes" in Christ."

And so through Him the "Amen" is spoken by us to the glory of God.

PRAYER: Father, thank You that You go before us; that You are making ever crooked places straight. That You put inside of me all that I need; that my prayers are heard and it creates change and movement for Your glory.

DECREE: I shall speak a thing and it shall come to pass. I shall speak a thing and it shall do what I send it to do. My words will achieve the purpose for which it was sent through Christ Jesus. I believe and have the faith for it.

Notes

DAY 15: SPEAK IT ... SAY IT ... PROPHESY

2 Corinthians 4:13 "It is written: 'I believed; therefore I have spoken.' With that same spirit of faith we also believe and therefore speak."

John 3:34 "For the one whom God has sent speaks the words of God, for God, gives the Spirit without limits."

God is giving you access to speak. This is truly our calling; your words frame your world; you have that much power to frame, reshape your life and destiny, order to your atmosphere by your word power. This can be activated by your voice, sending out commands, more than ever we are in a time where our voice moves mountains.

So let's think, we have all these electronic devices that are voice activated, responding to what we tell it to do, and it does, listening to our instructions, it is programed to deliver, to respond to requests immediately.

Well, guess Who had the program first? God invented it; we just can't see it or touch it, but it's listening and waiting to hear our voice to respond quickly. We don't actually see how our commands are delivered through our voice activated electronics, but it is delivered in the cyber world. Just know the same is applied with you and

God; we can't see, but our commands are delivered in the spirit realm. It's by faith that we operate. Not by sight but by faith, the things we cannot see but are hoped for.

John 3:34 "For the one whom God has sent speaks the words of God, for God gives the Spirit without limit."

1 Corinthians 14:3 "On the other hand, the one who prophesies speaks to people for their up building and encouragement and consolation."

There are prophets that are called by God in the office of a prophet, and then there's you. Paul said he wished all could prophesy and that we should desire the gift of prophecy.

1 Corinthians 14:1 "Follow the way of love and eagerly desire gifts of the Spirit, especially prophecy."

1 Corinthians 14:39 "Therefore, my brothers and sister, be eager to prophesy, and do not forbid speaking in tongues."

So, desire it, ask for the gifts of the Spirit of God to be released in your life. Activate by faith, and move forward in your word power. SPEAK IT! SAY IT! PROPHESY!

Romans 10:14-15 "How, then, can they call on the one they have not believed in? And how can they preach unless they are sent? As it is written, 'How beautiful are the feet of those who bring good news!'" (NKJV)

It is God's will for us to share the gospel. To share God's Word, in any given opportunity. No fear; God will lead you. He goes before you. He has already set and ordained the timing for you to share. Take it—don't miss it.

Romans 12:6 "Having gifts that differ according to the grace given to us, let us use them: if prophecy, in proportion to our faith; see what you say and say what you see, giving it life through the breath of God." (ESV)

1 Thessalonians 5:30 "Do not despise prophecies,"

John 6:63 "The Spirit gives life, the flesh counts for nothing. The words I have spoken to you—they are full of the Spirit and life."

Speak the fire of God into other lives and yours, a fresh wind of the Holy Spirit, a download of the supernatural provision, God's grace and mercy, for miracles to manifest.

Psalm 62:6 "Truly he is my rock and my salvation; he is my fortress, I will not be shaken."

QUESTION: Will you speak it, say it, and prophesy it, starting today? How will this help you?

PRAYER: Father, as we are in your image, help me to speak in faith; help me to use my voice to prophesy.

DECREE: I declare that I will speak—I will say it and I will prophesy life through the word of God.

Notes

DAY 16: PRAISES GO UP ... BLESSINGS COME DOWN

Psalm 119: 171-172 "May my lips overflow with praise, for you teach me your decrees. May my tongue sing of your words, for all your commands are righteous."

FYI—Blessings come with obedience.

Deuteronomy 28:1-3 "If you fully obey the LORD your God and carefully follow all his commands I give you today, the LORD your God will set you high above all the nations on earth. All these blessings will come on you and accompany you if you obey the LORD your God: You will be blessed in the city and blessed in the country."

There are many forms of praise. Whatever way God moves you to praise Him, follow the flow, be led by the Spirit or do what is needed to break forth and break out of your slumber or stagnant place that you may enter in to His presence.

Sometimes, we feel stuck with no movement or feel like we just can't do anything. This is the best way to break forth and to be set free of those snares of the enemy or the places that keep us bound, locked up and stuck. You never want to stay in that place for a long time.

You always want to break out immediately. Break out, praise and worship God.

God inhabits our praises. They are pleasing to Him in any language or tongue, when we are in the mist of praising. It's an exchange taking place. You give the Lord a song of worship, He takes your worship and then He gives to you. You send and He descends. (SINGING GREAT ARE YOU LORD!)

What is praise? It's an expression of one's respect and gratitude as an act of worship. It's truly a form of worship unto the Lord, singing, dancing, music, prayers. There are many other acts of worship unto the Lord as others have been creative with worshiping God. Don't put God in a box or use small thinking. Ask God to enlarge your territory, enlarge your paradigm, shift and elevate yourself to a new place in Him.

Psalm 150:6 "Let everything that has breath praise the Lord."

As we send up our praises, God releases strength, power, strategy, provision, answers prayers, healing, miracles, shifting, movement, change, forgiveness, joy, hope, peace, unity and love. Whatever your need is of God, He will fill that need. Just ask Him.

Deuteronomy 28:6 "You will be blessed when you come in and blessed when you go out."

QUESTION: Will you ask God to teach you how to praise and worship Him? How will this help you?

PRAYER: Lord, take us deeper, create in me true praise and worship that is pleasing unto You. Let my heart be full of praise and decrees that it continuously overflows from my mouth.

DECREE: I will praise you through it all. I will continue to worship You in spirit and truth. I will send my praise up with the expectation of change and blessings coming down. I know all things are working for my good because I love the Lord.

Notes

DAY 17: OPEN YOUR MOUTH

Psalm 81:10 "For it was I, the LORD your God, who rescued you from the land of Egypt. Open your mouth wide and I will fill it with good things." (NLT)

Do not be afraid to speak, but you may feel lost for words at times. This does not have to be! Scream ... open your mouth! Say it, speak it, do it, believe it! Your mouth is a weapon for tearing down strongholds, closing gates and opening doors, building and destroying, creating change. You can pull these things down from heaven; you have access. Access is granted to you.

This is a time more than ever when we need to hear your voice. The heavens and the earth need to hear your voice, your prayers to activate change. Change that starts with you by using your word power.

Matthew 18:18 "Truly I tell you, whatever you bind on earth will be bound in heaven, and whatever you loose on earth will be loosed in heaven."

There's a flow that can takes place, and God will fill your mouth as you take the first step and speak. The more you eat the Word of God, the easier it is to come out of your mouth. The more you read and study the Word and praise Him, living waters will flow from your tongue. What is in you will come out of you. Don't be lost in prayer; just ask God to fill your mouth and He will do it. Get quiet; let Him speak to your spirit. That is truly one of the best ways to be led by the Holy Spirit, praising God, worshipping God, talking to GOD. Prayer is key for entering into a deeper intimacy and relationship with God. His praise is forever on our lips.

Psalm 34:1 "I will praise the LORD at all times. I will constantly speak his praises." (NLT)

Matthew 21:16 "... and said to Him, 'Do you hear what these children are saying?'" they asked him. 'Yes,' replied Jesus, have you never read, 'From the lips of children and infants you, Lord have called forth praise?'"

QUESTION: Will you open your mouth and allow God to fill it? How will this help you?

PRAYER: God, I pray that when I open my mouth, you will fill it. Help me to walk in a new boldness with the reassurance that you are there speaking to me and through me.

DECREE: I will walk in a boldness and open my mouth to share Your Word, oh God. I will release blessing from heaven to earth in Jesus' name.

DAY 18: SPEAKING UP FOR OTHERS

Proverbs 31:8-9 "Speak up for those who cannot speak for themselves, for the right of all who are destitute. Speak up and judge fairly; defend the rights of the poor and needy."

Truly, this is my favorite. It warms my heart. What a blessing to speak for a mighty cause, to fight for others who do not have a voice. How much more can one give of themselves than by giving the power of their voice to the voiceless. This alone is so powerful, and it brings me great joy for those of you who are already using your voice to speak for others.

    Sometime in life we are born into a matter, having no choice; we didn't put ourselves there, but we definitely have to fight to get out. Others, we get knocked down, have setbacks and delays, and disappointment sets in over the course of time that causes us to become very tired and weary. We can't pray; we can't speak; and we can't see our way out of the storm. Then there are some whose voice simply cannot be heard, but thanks be to God that He makes intercession for us, and that He raises up a voice to speak on our behalf.

Romans 8:26 "In the same way, the Spirit helps us in our

weakness. We do not know what we ought to pray for, but the Spirit himself intercedes for us through wordless groans."

God fights for us. He fights our battles; He goes before us. He always prays for us or sends others to pray on our behalf. Thank God that He always sends others to strengthen us when we are weak. To fight for us when all the fight is gone; when we can't hear, see or speak, God sends help on our behalf.

I love that God has sent us to speak for others on the frontline. Fighting on the battlefield. You are a Chainbreaker, a change maker, game changer, a mover and a shaker. Step into what God has called you to—to be a voice for many through praying, an activist, philanthropist, leader, judge and much more; it doesn't matter what field or profession you're in. You have a voice, use it! We need your voice in this hour.

Job 16:21 "On behalf of a man he pleads with God as one pleads for a friend."

QUESTION: Will you ask God to help you speak up for others, judge fairly, and defend those who cannot for themselves? How will this help you?

PRAYER: Thank You, God, that You are with us; that you are a just GOD, a righteous God, a God Who help us to speak and fight for others rights with the righteousness of you, not man. Let us use our voice for great and mighty works for the advancement of the Kingdom of God, in Jesus' name.

DECREE: I will use my voice to speak for others, by the will of God with guidance, wisdom and truth. I will walk boldly with great courage, using my word power for God's righteousness, in Jesus' name.

Notes

DAY 19: TELL IT TO MOVE

MARK 11:23 "I tell you the truth, if anyone says to this mountain, 'Go, throw yourself into the sea,' and does not doubt in his heart but believes that what he says will happen, it will be done for him."

Who are you great mountain that you should not bow low? God is speaking to us through His Word to use and exercise our authority by using our words, tongue and our mouth, using our very own word power. Speaking to a thing that seems like in the natural is unmovable, but with God's authority it will move and it shall happen. We must operate in a greater faith.

Just as Jesus spoke to the fig tree and it withered and dried up. Jesus was a great example of exercising faith and authority. The disciples were blessed by witnessing such power and the authority of His words, which gave them an even greater faith and belief.

Matthew 21:19 "Seeing a fig tree by the road, he went up to it but found nothing on it except leaves, then he said to it, 'May you never bear fruit again!' Immediately the tree withered."

GOD has given us this same authority through His name, His Word, and the name of Jesus. Be mindful that we will one day run into setbacks, delays, failures, things that are beyond our control. This should push us to fight harder for more, pushing for more. There will always be something that comes our way that we did not welcome or invite. The surprise means that we must speak to it quickly, putting it under our feet, taking authority over it, redirecting, canceling, stopping it, with the name of Jesus. Pleading the blood of Jesus for protection; there's power in the blood, there's power in the name of King Jesus of Nazareth. There' power in His Word!

Jeremiah 23:29 "'Is not my word like fire,' declares the LORD, 'and like a hammer that breaks a rock to pieces?'"

Just image taking a hammer and breaking a rock. That is what your authority looks like. So whatever mountain you're facing, or trials and tribulations, speak to the rock, break it into pieces. Speak to the mountain, tell it to move by the authority Jesus has given to you, and do not doubt, but believe it will be done in Jesus' name.

QUESTION: Will you tell the obstacles that stand in your way to move starting today, using your word power, and saying to the things that are holding you up and delaying your blessing to move? How will this help you?

PRAYER: God activate my authority. Impart in me the new thing; give me a new revelation of my authority from/

in you. Help me to use it to speak to obstacles that stand in my way in Jesus' name.

DECREE: I will use my authority to speak to mountains in my life and in others' lives and it shall move. I will walk in all that You have given me and believe it shall be done in Jesus' name.

Notes

DAY 20: HEALING WORDS

Psalm 107:20 "He sent out his word and healed them; he rescued them from the grave."

Psalm 147:3 "He heals the broken hearted and binds up their wounds."

God is a healer. He is a restoration God. Jehovah-Rapha ... The God Who heals! The Word of God is truly healing; it is a Word unlike any other. It is one-on-one counseling therapy, self-help, motivational, Instructional, growth and development, anger management, anxiety cure, a depression breaker. It heals the mind, the soul, the body and the heart, right down to your very bones.

God has put healing words in your mouth and heart and Spirit led words to speak and release into one another. What God has, you have access to. Use YOUR WORD POWER as healing words, communicating and recognizing others greatness that may never have been revealed before. Plow your way in and find what is good, then speak it, saying ... your beautiful, your awesome at what you do, I appreciate you, great job. Do you need any help? Thank you!

Small, kind gestures can be healing to one's soul. It can be an awakening, letting one know their self-worth. That they are appreciated, accepted, respected and loved.

Sometimes, people really are not aware of who they truly are, not knowing their full potential until someone like you, reveals it. This can truly make the world a better place if we start using our word power for healing the brokenhearted, the sick and the wounded, healing the spiritually dead, bringing them back from the dust to life.

Starting today with you and your word power, will you use it to heal? I encourage you to start taking baby steps and grow from there. Even in prayer, God has given us healing prayers and healing power, the authority to heal the sick and raise the dead, heal the land and nation, heal our family and loved ones.

As you pray for someone, the atmosphere begins to shift. Change is taking place. You invite the Lord in and let the Holy Spirit fill the room. Have faith and receive, in Jesus' name.

Have you ever longed for an apology or affirmation from someone? You feel that if that would happen, things would be much better in your life. Only to find out that was not the truth. It's deeper than that. Maybe a certain person never said I love you or I am sorry, or asked can you please forgive me?

Just as you may long to hear words that bring comfort and peace, so do other people. We are emotional beings. We live better when we are interactive with one another, taking care of each other in small ways. Let GOD began to heal you and your heart. He knows exactly how to fix the broken pieces and what you need to be restored, so that you may heal others. Ask the Lord to enlarge your territory that you may begin healing a nation by your tongue, by your word power.

Proverbs 12:18 "The words of the reckless pierce like swords, but the tongue of the wise bring healing."

QUESTION: Will you ask God to give you the Faith to heal, using your word power? How will this help you?

PRAYER: Father God, heal us with Your Word. Help us to speak healing words to one another and build our faith for Your miracles.

DECREE: I will use my words as healing words to the broken and wounded. I decree my words will heal nations. My words will heal, placing peace love and joy in one's heart in Jesus' name.

Notes

DAY 21: BUILDING WORDS

Ephesians 4:29 "Do not let any unwholesome talk come out of your mouths, but only what is helpful for building others up according to their needs, that it may benefit those who listen."

1 Thessalonians 5:11 "Therefore encourage one another and build one another up, just as you are doing. Just as^2 you would take a building block and take one block at a time to build a strong foundation, you know every piece has been set firm strategically place with love and care." (ESV)

Build others up around you; build up your leaders, friends, loved ones and even strangers. You may under-estimate how needed and uplifting this can be for others. Have you ever used your words to build and uplift others? Then they share with you how that was exactly what they needed to hear, how it blessed them, how they feel new, a release and a confidence. Sometimes, we can truly loose our identity, experiencing a low in life, holding our head down. We just need someone to lift up our head when it's hanging low; rise up—rise up child of God.

You may be hiding or have decided to isolate yourself, but no one can hide from God. He knows your exact GPS location. He can reach you and see you. He is there; He has never left you and those words will find you whether it's in a song, TV, media, man or woman. When God is ready, It will happen. Know those building words can set people free, break chains off, give one new life, a fresh wind, a fresh breath. A new heartbeat. I know you want to be a part of that, so I encourage you to start today using your words to build.

Lift up your head; lift up your eyes; its time to rise from the dust and receive your reward. I enjoy seeing something being built. It's a fresh and new creation, no limitations on the design. The growth is beyond measure.

Romans 14:19 "Let us therefore make and mutual edification."

Proverbs 27:17 "Iron sharpens iron, and one man sharpens another." (ESV)

This is what we are called to do as children of God. To build, build His Kingdom and His Kingdom people, our brothers and sisters.

2 Corinthians 13:11 "Finally, brother and sisters, rejoice! Strive for full restoration, encourage one another, be of one mind, live in peace. And the God of love and peace will be with you."

Romans 14:19 "Let us therefore make every effort to do what leads to peace and to mutual edification."

QUESTION: Will you start using your word power to build others, building for the Kingdom of God? How will this help you?

PRAYER: Father God, fill my mouth with building words—words that hit the mark, that penetrate the hearts of man. Jesus is my rock for which I stand for Your glory in Jesus' na me.

DECREE: I will use my words to build. I will build a strong foundation for God's glory. I will use words to build and not words to tear down others.

Notes

Day 22: SWEET WORDS

Proverbs 16:24 "Pleasant words are like a honeycomb, Sweetness to the soul and health to the bones." (NKJV)

Proverbs 15:4 "The soothing tongue is a tree of life, but a perverse tongue crushes the spirit.

Proverbs 12:25 "An anxious heart weighs a man down, but a kind word cheers him up." (NLT)

We all need a kind word. We deserve sweet words. We desire affirmation of who we really are. We need occasional reminders of who we are called to be in Christ Jesus. We need confirmation and reassurance; that's normal that our spirit longs for these words. Truly it is much needed food for the soul, but there's not enough of it going around.
    Daily we can experience such a negative and toxic environment that we began to feel drained. We must shake off the dust quickly. We have so many words that are not positive or productive, but those of destruction. Words can stick to us, making us sticky sticker?, weighing us down, making our thoughts and our heart heavy. Our thoughts can be so heavy that we can't even see or move any more. Our vision slowly disappears or dissolves slowly, floating away.
    But God has called us to love and to speak life into

each other. It is a command! To love, build and encourage one another.

Matthew 22:39 "And a second is like it: you shall love your neighbor as yourself." (NKJV)

This is God's desire for us to spread love, even to the unloveable. Speaking words that are sweeter than honey, kind words, filling words, life words, loving words, rhema words, and Spirit-led words. May the sweet Word of the Lord fill our mouths to bring joy, hope, peace, unity and love in the earth.

Have you ever had someone speak to you with such a sweet word on their tongue that it entered straight into your heart? It was so sweet that you truly felt it. It melted your heart, knowing those words were God's love speaking to you, imparting a new strength and hope. Its effect is strong and sometimes ever-lasting, opening places in your heart that may have been closed by you, not being able to receive or give the true love God desires for us to experience.

But God's love is inevitable. It's God's sweet words that breaks down walls, breaks through barriers, kicks and knocks down doors. God's love fights for you. His love is chasing after you, carrying a fragrance of sweetness, freshness and wholeness, planting strong roots. These words enter into the soul, the bones, these words are truly transformational words. What an aroma to set in the atmosphere—transforming words, restoring words. It's pleasant, peaceful and charming words that lift, build and remove burdens awakening life. God wants you free from any bondage of words that may have trapped you in a place, space or time. Receiving sweet words lifts your spirt. What a pleasant and gratifying experience that brings you joy and fulfillment. Know the seed has been planted and it's taking root to grow. It's all well, rewarding and worth it, planting these sweet harvest of seeds. It will not cost you anything but the reward is great as you are spreading goodness and sweetness across the globe.

Psalm 34:8 "Taste and see that the LORD is Good; blessed is the one who takes refuge in him."

QUESTION: What sweet words, and affirmations, will you speak today, starting and using with your word power? How will this help you?

PRAYER: God you are my beloved, what would I do without Your goodness and mercy? I ask You to fill my mouth with sweet words that I may bless others with just a taste of Your goodness in Jesus' name.

DECREE: I am releasing sweet words into the world, the atmosphere, into people, the heavens, and unto You, God. My words will be kind-loving, heart-filling. My words will be used to impart the love of God, in Jesus' name.

Notes

DAY 23: WISDOM

Proverbs 10:31 "The mouth of the righteous bring forth wisdom, but a perverse tongue will be cut out." (ESV)

Proverbs 2:6 "For the LORD gives wisdom; from his mouth come knowledge and understanding;"

Proverbs 8:11 "For wisdom is more precious than rubies, and nothing you desire can compare with her."

Proverbs 18:4 "The words of the mouth are deep waters, but the fountains of wisdom is a rushing stream."

The definition of Wisdom is: "the quality of having experience, knowledge, and good judgment; quality of being wise." God-given wisdom is supernatural; it is Spirit led, being led by the Holy Spirit, which takes you higher than your own natural wisdom. Choose God's wisdom to take you higher and further then you could ever imagine.
    Speaking in wisdom, talking and walking in wisdom so much so that others recognize it. When people see you, they're like wishing for a moment of your time for your insight, overview and very wise council. They value your thoughts, views, perspective and judgment. Just one conversation with you brings peace and lots of clarity. They know your charter is for the Kingdom of God and His righteous.

1 Corinthians 2:9 "However, as it is written: 'What no eyes has seen, or ear has heard, and what no human mind has conceived the things God has prepared for those who love him.'"

God's wisdom is bigger than we could ever imagine and God wants you to be blessed beyond measure. He wants you to think outside of the box with no limitations on your life. His wisdom will take you higher and higher.

James 1:5 "If any of you lack wisdom, you should ask God, who gives generously to all without finding fault, and it will be given to you."

Just ask God; He will give you all that you need. Surely, God wants us to speak with wisdom being led by the Holy Spirit. His wisdom is one of the many gifts that God has given to us.

QUESTION: Will you ask God for wisdom today? How will this help you?

PRAYER: God you are majestic in all your ways. I bless Your name, Father. I am asking for wisdom and knowledge in my life, that I will see and understand the value of them both and operate in the fullness of You and all that you have ordained me to be, in Jesus' name.

DECREE: I will walk in wisdom and God-given wisdom to complete great exploits for Your glory. I will speak in wisdom being led by the Holy Spirit.

Notes

DAY 24: KNOWLEDGE

Proverbs 15:2 "The tongue of the wise adorns knowledge, but the mouth of the fool gushes folly."

Proverbs 10:14 "The wise store up knowledge but the mouth of a fool invites ruin."

Hosea 4:6 "My people are destroyed from lack of knowledge."

2 Peter 1:3 "His divine power has given us everything we need for a godly life through our knowledge of him."

Proverbs 17:27 "The one who has knowledge uses words with restraint, and whoever has understanding is even tempered."

God wants us to retain knowledge, and through Him we have full access. The keys are yours—open the door, walk through it by faith. When you ask by faith, you receive. As knowledge flows off of your tongue, it blesses others to no measure. It's something you cannot buy, but it isn't free. It comes with a cost called experience, trials and tribulations, walking through the fire. You cannot teach it if you didn't go through it. You made it through to talk about it and share it to be a blessing you are for many.

Knowledge is power. We live in a world today where knowing is at the touch of a fingertip; knowledge is more accessible than ever before. Obtaining information is our new normal; it's everywhere. Knowledge is a must for growth and development. I am a huge fan of self-help books and the Bible is the number 1# best-seller in the world. It has all the help you can ever need. But the key is you have to open it, and read it, study it, and meditate on it day and night. I guarantee you, you will never be the same as you study the Word of God. The Word of God is a living word, live and active.

This is a world full of knowledge and God wants us to obtain the truth, and knowledge of Him. God teaches in His Word, my people are destroyed from the lack of knowledge, so don't reject knowledge. Ask for it, pray for it, know that God want us to continually learn and grow. If you're not growing you're dying. Times change every day. Don't stay the same—stuck in your old ways. God does new things, in new ways, but He stays the same because He is God.

Proverbs 1:7 "The fear of the Lord is the beginning of knowledge; fool despise wisdom and instruction."

QUESTION: Will you ask God for the gift of knowledge today? How will this help you?

PRAYER: God, thank You, for giving us all we need through You. When we ask, we receive in Jesus' name.

DECREE: I decree that I will go after knowledge, that I will seek Your face, Lord, for breakthrough after breakthrough. Victory after Victory. Blessing after Blessing. Shout! I am a conqueror through Christ Jesus.

Notes

DAY 25: SELF-CONTROL

2 Timothy 1:7 "For God did not give us a spirit of timidity, but a spirit of power, of love and self-discipline." (NLT)

James 3:2 "For we all stumble in many ways, And if anyone does not stumble in what he says, he is a perfect man, able also to bridle his whole body." (ESV)

Self-control does not come overnight. It takes hard work. It takes a new mindset. It takes discipline. But it can be done—starting with you making a choice for positive change that will last a lifetime, having self-control of what you say and speak takes discipline. Do you want it or not? If you want it, God will give it to you. God will help you get there. Just ask Him. What you may think is impossible ... may be ... because you did not ask for help.

Mark 9:23 "And Jesus said to him, 'If you can believe, all things are possible for one who believes."

So, ask and believe and receive in Jesus' name. Even staying pure until marriage, making a choice to be abstinent and celibate is not easy. You truly need God's help every day until you're walking in His strength and protection. But it's also better to marry then burn. So if you struggle with this, keep seeking God and a godly mentor or leader for wise council and direction. God is there for you. He has every answer you need, every road map to direct you out of sin and into a blessed lifestyle.

Hebrews 12:11 "No discipline seems pleasant at the time, but painful. Later on, however, it produces a harvest of righteousness and peace for those who have been trained by it."

There's a great reward in being disciplined and practicing self-control. Your discipline is your reward. Say this out loud ... I will not let other things control me. I will control me—my thoughts, my emotions, my mind, my body, and my actions. Self-control reflects all areas of your life that are vital to a life of excellence, and you, yes you, want to walk in a spirit of excellence. We want every good thing God has for us.

Proverbs 25:28 "A man without self-control is like a city broken into and left without walls." (ESV)

Self-control can bring you much favor in your life. Have you ever seen a person receive opportunity after opportunity because other people admire there self-control and discipline? They see that person was reliable and has accountability, is trustworthy, has great morals, values and character. It will open numerous doors for you, guaranteed. So let's practice self-control, fighting our flesh to obtain all God has for us.

QUESTION: Will you ask GOD to help you with self-control? Will you apply self-control to your life this week? How will this help you?

PRAYER: Father God, help me to practice self-control. Impart in me the strength to walk in self-control and discipline. Help me to have a disciplined tongue. Help me to have self-control in all areas of my life.

DECREE: I will walk in a God-given strength of self-control and discipline. I rebuke anything that stands in my way in Jesus' name.

Notes

DAY 26: WAIT

Proverbs 18:13 "He who answers before listening—that is his folly and his shame."

James 1:19 "My dear brothers, take note of this: Everyone should be quick to listen, slow to speak and slow to become angry."

Psalm 27:14 "Wait for the LORD; be strong and take heart and wait for the LORD."

The definition of wait is: Caution; Care taken to avoid danger or mistakes. We must practice waiting, listening and hearing to gain an understanding of what is ... before speaking. This represents our relationship with God and others, knowing God's timing is key for movement before you act or respond.

This is a safe place to exercise for you and others, to wait, you never know what a person is experiencing or going through, and your response could be detrimental to one's life choices. We must act with caution and love. The question is: Can you wait, and will you wait, especially when it is a tight and narrow place? We all get weary of waiting, but God is with us.

Isaiah 40:31 "But they that wait upon the Lord shall renew

their strength; they shall mount up with wings as eagles; they shall run and not be weary; and they shall walk, and not faint." (ESV)

Philippians 4:6 "Do not be anxious about anything, but in every situation, by prayer and petition, with thanksgiving, present your request to God."

Let's put this into practice ASAP. Let's wait before speaking, before our prayer requests unto God. Let's wait on using our word power that it may be used effectively and safely with caution and care and most importantly love. Waiting is key to your word power.

QUESTION: Will you ask God to help you to wait? How will this help you?

PRAYER: Father God, help me to wait and use caution when responding to others. Help me to operate with love and understanding as a representative of You. Let the Holy Spirit operate in me fully. I invite You, Holy Spirit into my life to move freely. Teach me patience, understanding, compassion and love, just to be a hearing ear to someone. I will be that one that maybe someone is in need of.

DECREE: I will wait on the Lord. I will listen. I will hear before I speak or respond to others. I will use wisdom, love, compassion and understanding as I use my God-given word power in Jesus' name.

DAY 27: THE RIGHT ANSWER

Colossians 4:6 "Let your conversation be always full of grace, seasoned with salt, so that you may know how to answer everyone."

Proverbs 16:1 "To humans belong the plans of the heart, but from the LORD comes the proper answer of the tongue."

Truly, we all have given a wrong answer or have had a wrong response. How do you fix it? Maybe quit? We must be teachable.

Job 6:24 "Teach me, and I will be quiet; show me where I have been wrong."

Not truly knowing how we have effected someone's life or matter is important. Something can be as life-changing as making them do or don't, stay or leave. It is critical that we think about how important giving the right answer is, especially at the right time. So at times, the right answer is no answer. You don't have to have an answer to give a right one.

Have you ever experienced looking for answers and a response and that person wouldn't give it to you? Trust and know they were truly using wisdom, and you found the right answer within yourself, as you trusted God for His provision and wisdom.

Romans 8:31 "What, then shall we say in response to this? If God is for us, who can be against us?"

What a great example of the right answer. Always pause, ponder and pray before you give an answer or response. Giving God time to humble our hearts, allow Him to speak to us before moving forward. We always do not make the right decision or choices, but we must seek God first for every move we make and every step we take, whether it is our life or others.

Proverbs 15:23 "A man hath joy by the answer of his mouth, and a word spoken in due season—how good is it!" (NKJV)

Let us be full of grace and be the salt of the earth, meaning some flavor and life. Maybe the right answer could be in no answer at all. Example: "I don't have an answer for that" or "Let me think about it," or "Can I get back to you on that?" Sleep on it; rest on it before boldly blurting out something, even if it was your first thought. Just be safe and wait for the answer.

QUESTION: Will you ask God to help you and to give you the right answers? How will this help you?

PRAYER: God, our Heavenly Father, please help me starting today to pause, ponder and pray before responding. Give me heavenly wisdom for the right answer, at the right moment, and the right time for the right season in Jesus' name.

DECREE: I will seek God first and I will wait on you, God, for the right answer and the right timing in Jesus' name.

Notes

DAY 28: DON'T COMPLAIN

Philippians 2:14 "Do everything without complaining or arguing."

James 5:9 "Do not grumble against one another, brothers so that you may not be judged; behold the Judge is standing at the door!" (ESV)

I do not want any more delays or setbacks in my life because of my mouth or what I speak or say. What should have taken the children of Israel 11 days, took 40 years, as they wandered in the wilderness, complaining on their journey to the Promise Land.

    The Bible teaches us so much. It's truly the greatest road map in life. So much loss for the children of Israel because of complaining. This is a harsh consequence, but God is showing us a great example of how He doesn't approve of complaining. Let's digest this to get a clear understanding of how important this is. This is serious business with God. Repeat after me ... "My great God, Who loves and blesses my life, supplying all of my needs before I even know what I need."

    God does not want me to complain. He does not like it, and He will not tolerate it! Just as in life, we don't find it pleasing when our kids complain, etc. We are disappointed and saddened, but we still fight for them, hoping one day all truths are revealed. We carry forth, trying to change their views, values, and morals until they gain an understanding, and with an unconditional love, we love them trying to guide them on the right path. We truly want nothing but the best for them. We want them to fly higher than we ever did, dreaming big. We want the fullness and their greatest potential to manifest in their life. We want God's will to bloom forth in fullness in their life. That's truly a parents' heart for their children.

It really rubs us the wrong way when our kids are ungrateful or someone in our life that has no understanding has no gratitude. That's how our Abba Father in heaven feels.

Find a new away to redirect those thoughts, feelings and emotions. Please give them all to God. Lay them at His feet. If you just say a quiet prayer to God to help you redirect those emotions and feelings, God will help you. Peace be still.

Quietly you can ask, "God help my views, my thoughts, my feelings and my emotions on a daily basis, so that I will operate in a positive and pleasing manner unto you."

Thessalonians 5:18 "Give thanks in all circumstances; for this is the will of God in Christ Jesus for you." (ESV)

QUESTION: "Will you ask God to help you not complain, but give thanks in all circumstances? How will this help you?

PRAYER: I repent, Lord, for complaining. Forgive me, Father, for not keeping my eyes on you in matters when I feel overwhelmed, discouraged, and doubtful or just not seeing the bigger picture, vision, or for not seeing Your hand, molding my life. I pray that You shift me into a new strength that this will not be a part of my journey any more. To You I pray in Jesus' name.

DECREE: I will not use my mouth to complain. I will use it unto the Lord to rejoice and give praises and thanks in all circumstances.

Notes

DAY 29: DON'T LIE

Proverbs 12:22 "The Lord detest lying lips, but he delights in people who are trustworthy."

Proverbs 12:19 "Truthful lips endure forever but a lying tongue lasts only a moment."

Psalm 34:13 "Keep your tongue from evil and your lips from telling lies."

John 14:15 "If you love me, keep my commands."

Psalm 119:172 "May my tongue sing of your word, for all your commands are righteous."

The Ten Commandments tell us not to be a false witness against thy neighbor. This means don't go around spreading lies against one another, causing confliction. Do not do it. God does not like it. He detests it—dislikes it intensely! Do not Lie, Period! It's just not cool. It causes harm, hurt and pain, and most importantly, distrust. Lying only leaves a trail to ruins that one has to try to fix. A lie is more costly to fix then it is to tell it.

    Many justify why they may have told a lie, to protect another from harm or hurt or themselves. Like Abraham lied to the king that his wife Sarah was his sister because he was afraid, which almost brought destruction to the king. (Genesis 20:1-13). Is a lie justified?

They are a million reasons that a lie can be told, but one will only have to seek God for direction and the wisdom that leads to the truth. Seek God for the freedom that one may be held in bondage to from telling a lie or being lied to. Lies are just too costly for both parties. It is a price you will pay one day. So let's be cautious about our actions. Understand we do not go digging up old dirt and old wounds without wise council. Some things are best left alone, and some are not. Needing answers and searching for the truth, isn't always an easy route. It takes courage to be truthful when the truth can cost you everything.

We all have lied once or twice in our lives, but moving forward let us be who God has called us to be, operating in the spirit of truth.

Proverbs 10:18 "Whoever conceals hatred with lying lips and spreads slander is a fool."

Leviticus 19:11 "Do not steal. Do not lie. Do not deceive one another."

QUESTION: Will you ask God to help you to do what is only pleasing to Him? How will this help you?

PRAYER: God, I repent for any lie that I have ever told. Forgive me for my lying tongue. Cleanse my mouth. Help me to walk with a truthful tongue, building trust and honesty. I pray that everyone is healed from a lie or lies that have caused them hurt and harm in Jesus' name.

DECREE: I will use my words, my lips, my mouth, my tongue in truthfulness, trust and honesty.

Notes

DAY 30: DON'T GOSSIP—NOT COOL

Proverbs 18:8 "The word of a gossip are like choice morsels; they go down to a man's inmost parts."

Proverbs 11:13 "A gossip betrays a confidence, but a trustworthy person keeps a secret."

Gossip is anything being repeated that was spoken in a private, confidential way and spoken in trust. Note: one should not have to ask for a conversation to be kept confidential; it should be a given and an unspoken rule. You want a reputation of trust, so that one can trust you with secrets of their heart that you will submit only to the Father in prayer. Everyone needs someone they can trust to talk to, vent to, bounce ideas and views off of. Everyone needs that someone. Let's pray you can be that someone, and that God sends that someone into your life ... a friend or confidant that will be trustworthy and wise.

    A new word for today is loyalty. Loyalty is something we may all have forgotten about, but look up the definition. Even pillow talk with your spouse is breaking the trust of a friend. You would need to ask for permission from that person if it is okay to share this with my husband or wife if more council was needed. Let's be wise as God's children.

Ecclesiastes 10:20 "Do not revile the king even in your thoughts, or curse the rich in your bedroom, because a bird in the sky may carry your words, and a bird on the wing may report what you say."

Proverbs 17:9 "Whoever would foster love covers over an offense, but whoever repeats the matter separates close friends."

QUESTION: Will ask God to help you hold your tongue from gossip? How will this help you?

PRAYERS: Father, forgive me for I have participated in some way or form in gossip. I repent to You for those I may have hurt with breaking such trust. I pray, Lord, that they are healed from my immature behavior, and they are released from any wounds I may have caused.

DECREE: I will not participate in any form of gossip. I will shut it down by the words of my mouth, saying 'STOP' that's not okay. I will change the conversation or shut it down. I will not participate in tea time so my interest will not be in another's privacy. I decree I will be trustworthy unto my Father, keeping my mouth shut.

DAY 31: BLESS THEM

Romans 12:14 "Bless those who persecute you, Bless and do not curse."

Romans 12:12 "Rejoice in hope, be patient in tribulation, be constant in prayer."

Persecution will come, and then what? You must stand! Wipe off the dust; wipe those ugly words off of you. They do not belong to you. They are not yours; do not receive them. Cancel the assignment of those words immediately.
    This will happen, but how do you handle it? Bless them! They persecuted our Lord and Savior Jesus Christ as He died on the cross for our sins that we may be free, so why not you? Especially when you are called to great works for the Kingdom of God. You will experience warfare, because there's an enemy that doesn't want you to win; he wants to fight you every step of the way. His mission is to stop you from getting to your next level in life, hoping you give up, hoping you throw in the towel, hoping he can blind you to not see your vision anymore. You need to know he will not stop.
    So why would you think it would be easy when you have so much destiny in your life? Anything worth having, is worth fighting for. We must fight the good fight of faith in Jesus' name. God will teach you how to fight and stand.

Do not curse those who persecute you; don't even think about it. Fight off those ugly emotions and thoughts. Be set free of any anger, rage and revenge. Go to God in prayer and let the Holy Spirit speak to your heart. Allow Him to soften your heart. So you can move forward in peace and freedom.

Matthew 5:9 "Blessed are the peacemakers, for they will be called children of God."

Colossians 3:23 "Whatever you do, work at it with all your heart, as working for the Lord, not for human masters."

Be set free! Don't become captive in bondage. Don't let someone else have that much control over you and who you are and whose you are.

Isaiah 54:17 "No weapon formed against you shall prosper, and every tongue which rises against you in judgment You shall condemn. This is the heritage of the servants of the Lord, and their righteousness is from Me," Says the LORD." (NKJV)

Philippians 4:4 "Rejoice in the Lord always; again I will say, Rejoice."

QUESTION: Will you start today taking the higher road to bless others who persecute you? How will this help you?

PRAYER: Father, help me to rise higher, teach me to bless others, even when they persecute me. Help me to bless them even when I know their heart and it's hard for me or when I am hurting or disappointed and it may seem like I am at the end of my rope. Take the lead in my heart, God, that I may release them to you, so that I can bless them.

DECREE: I will bless those who persecute me. I will give my hardened heart to God. I will bless them beyond measure in Jesus' name.

Notes

TARGET PRAYERS FOR YOU AND YOUR FAMILY

- FREE FROM FEAR
- FREE FROM LUST
- FREE FROM SIN
- FREE FROM SICKNESS AND DISEASE
- FREE FROM HOPE DEFERRED, DOUBT
- FREE FROM BONDAGE BREAKING CHAINS
- FREE FROM CONFUSION AND DELUSION
- FREE FROM THE FEAR OF DEATH
- FREE FROM CONFLICT, STRIFE
- FREE FROM PROVERTY, LACK
- PRAYERS FOR FAMILYCHILDREN, SPOUSE, SILBLINGS
- PRAYERS FOR YOUR CITY / STATE / GOVERNMENT
- PRAYERS FOR OUR PRESIDENT / LEADERSHIP / CITY OFFICIALS / SCHOOLS / CHURCH / WORKPLACE
- PRAYERS FOR THE ECONOMY
- PRAYERS FOR THE ENVIRONMENT / AIR QUALITY

- PRAYERS FOR PRISIONS / HOMELESS / ORPHANS AND WIDOWS
- PRAYERS FOR THE NATIONS AND ISRAEL
- PRAYERS FOR UNITY / HOPE AND LOVE / FORGIVENESS / PEACE / UNDERSTANDING / RESTORATION
- PRAYERS FOR GROW IN CHRIST / TRUST / FAITH
- PRAYERS TO GIVE / GIVE BACK
- PRAYERS FOR THE NEXT GENERATION
- PRAYERS FOR YOUR FRIENDS AND NEIGHBORS

ABOUT THE AUTHOR

Robin Thompson has been called by God to share His Word. As she is walking into her destiny and purpose, she has received a call to release her first book. The Spirit of God has led her to share on using the power of your own words.

Dedicated and devoted to the King of kings, it is in her heart to share the Gospel, set the captives free, and empower and encourage God's people.

Robin has two sons and lives in Dallas, Texas.

To contact Robin go to:

Robin-Thompson.org